Enid Blyton's

· BIBLE · STORIES ·

THE THREE WISE MEN
& THE ANGEL'S WARNING

NEW TESTAMENT

GRAFTON BOOKS

A Division of the Collins Publishing Group

LONDON GLASGOW
TORONTO SYDNEY AUCKLAND

THE THREE WISE MEN

F ar far away from Bethlehem in a land that lay to the east, there lived some wise and learned men. At night these men studied the stars in the heavens. They said that the stars showed them the great thoughts of God. They said that when a new star appeared, it was God's way of telling men that some great thing was happening in the world.

Then, one night, a new star appeared in the sky, when the wise men were watching. The second night the star was brighter still. The third night it was so dazzling that its light seemed to put out the twinkling of the other stars.

"God has sent this star to say that something wonderful is happening," said the wise men. "We will look in our old, old book, where wisdom is kept, and we will find out what this star means."

So they studied their old wise books, and they found in them a tale of a great King who was to be born into the world to rule over it. He was to be King of the Jews, and ruler of the world.

"The star seems to stand over Israel, the kingdom of the Jews," said one wise man. "This star must mean that the great King is born at last. We will go to worship Him, for our books say He will be the greatest King in the world."

"We will take Him presents of gold and frankincense and myrrh," said another. "We will tell our servants to make ready to go with us."

So, a little while later, when the star was still brilliant every night in the sky, the three wise men set off on their camels. They were like kings in their own country, and a long train of servants followed behind on swift-footed camels. They travelled for many days and nights, and always at night the great star shone before them to guide them on their way.

They came at last to the land of Israel, where the little Jesus had been born. They went, of course, to the city where the Jewish King lived, thinking that surely the new little King would be there, in the palace of Jerusalem.

Herod was the king there, and he was a wicked man. When his servants came running to tell him that three rich men, seated on magnificent camels, with a train of servants behind them, were at the gates of the palace, Herod bade his servants bring them before him.

The wise men went to see Herod. They looked strange and most kingly in their turbans and flowing robes. They asked Herod a question that amazed and angered him.

"Where is the child who is born King of the Jews?" they asked. "His star has gone before us in the east, and we wish to worship Him. Where is He?"

"I am the King," said Herod, full of anger. "What is this child you talk of? And what is this star?"

The wise men told him all they knew. "We are certain that a great King has been born," they said, "and we must find Him. Can you not tell us where He is?"

Herod sat silent for a moment. Who was this new-born king these rich strangers spoke of? Herod was quite certain they were speaking the truth. He could see that these men were learned, and knew far more than he did.

"I will find out where this newborn King is, and kill him," thought Herod to himself. "But this I will not tell these men. They shall go to find the child for me, and tell me where he is—then I will send my soldiers to kill him."

So Herod spoke craftily to the wise men. "I will find out what you want to know. I have wise men in

my court who know the sayings of long-ago Jews, who said that in due time a great King would be born. Perhaps this is the child you mean."

Then Herod sent for his own wise men and

bade them look in the books they had to see what was said of a great King to be born to the Jews. The learned men looked and they found what they wanted to know.

"The King will be born in the city of Bethlehem," they said.

"Where is that?" asked the wise men.

"Not far away," said Herod. "It will not take you long to get there."

"We will go now," said the three wise men, and they turned to go. But Herod stopped them.

"Wait," he said, "when you find this new-born King, come back here to tell me where he is, for I too would worship him."

The wise men did not know that Herod meant to kill the little King, and not to worship Him. "You shall be told where He is," they said. "We will return here and tell you."

Then they mounted their camels and went to find the city of Bethlehem, which, as Herod had said, was not far away.

The sun set, and once again the brilliant star flashed into the sky. It seemed to stand exactly over the town of Bethlehem. The strangers, with their train of servants, went up the hill to Bethlehem, their harness jingling and their jewelled turbans and cloaks flashing in the brilliant light of the great star.

They passed the wondering shepherds, and went into the little city. They stopped to ask a woman to guide them.

"Can you tell us where to find a new-born child?" they asked.

The woman stared at these rich strangers in surprise. She felt sure they must want to know where Jesus was, for everyone knew how angels had come to proclaim His birth.

"Yes," she said, "you will find the baby in the house yonder. He was born in the stable of the inn, because there was no room for Him—but now that the travellers have left the city, room was found for His parents at that house. You will find Him there

with His mother."

The star seemed to stand right over the house to which the woman pointed. The wise men felt sure it was the right one. They made their way to it, riding on their magnificent camels.

THE ANGEL'S WARNING

When Mary saw these three grandly dressed men kneeling before her tiny baby, she was amazed. Angels had come to proclaim His birth, shepherds had worshipped Him—and now here were three great men kneeling before Him.

"We have found the little King," said one wise man. "We have brought Him kingly presents. Here is gold for Him, a gift for a King."

"And here is sweet-smelling frankincense," said another.

"And I bring Him myrrh, rare and precious," said the third. These were indeed kingly gifts, and Mary looked at them in wonder, holding the baby closely against her. He was her own child, but He seemed to belong to many others too—to the angels in heaven, to the simple shepherds in the fields, to wise and rich men of far countries. He had been born for the whole world, not only for her.

The wise men left and went to stay for the night at the inn. There was room for them, because the many travellers who had come to the little city had

left some time before.

"Tomorrow we will go back to Herod and tell him where the new-born King is, so that he may come and worship Him," said the wise men. But in the night God sent dreams to them, to warn them not to return to Herod, but to go back to their country another way.

So they mounted their camels, and returned to their country without going near Jerusalem, where Herod lived.

In vain Herod waited for the three wise men to return. His servants soon found out that they had been to Bethlehem but had returned home another way. This made Herod so angry that he hardly knew what he was doing.

First he sent his soldiers after the wise men to stop them, but they were too far away. Then he made up his mind to find the new-born baby and kill Him.

But no-one knew where the child was, nor did anyone even know how old He might be. The wise men themselves had not known how old the baby was. Herod sat on his throne, his heart black and angry.

"Call my soldiers to me," he said at last.

They came before him, and Herod gave them a cruel and terrible command.

"Go to the town of Bethlehem and kill every boy-child there who is under two years old," he said. "Go to the villages round about and kill the young baby-boys there too. Let no-one escape."

The soldiers rode off, their harness jingling loudly. They rode up the hill to Bethlehem, and once again the quiet shepherds stared in wonder at strange visitors. But soon, alas, they heard the screams and cries of the mothers whose little sons had been killed, and they knew that something dreadful was happening.

Every boy-child was killed by the cruel
soldiers, and when their terrible work was done,

they rode down the hills again, past the watching shepherds, to tell Herod that his commands had been obeyed.

"There is no boy-child under two years old left in Bethlehem or the villages nearby," said the

captain of the soldiers, and Herod was well pleased.

"The new-born King is dead," he thought. "I have been clever, I have killed the baby who might one day have been greater than I am."

But Jesus was not killed. He was safe. On the night that the wise men had left Mary, the little family had gone to bed, and were asleep. But, as Joseph slept, an angel came to him in his dreams, and spoke to him.

"Arise," said the shining angel. "Take the young Child and His mother, and flee into Egypt, and stay there until I tell you to return; for Herod will seek the young Child to destroy Him."

Joseph awoke at once. He sat up. The angel was gone, but the words he had said still sounded in Joseph's ears. Joseph knew that there was danger near, and he awoke Mary at once.

"We must make ready and go," he said, and

he told her what the angel had said. Then Mary knew they must go, and she went to put her few things into a bundle, and to lift up the baby Jesus. Joseph went to get the little donkey, and soon, in the silence of the night, the four of them fled away secretly.

They went as quickly as they could, longing to pass over into the land of Egypt, which did not belong to Herod. He would have no power over them there.

So, when Herod's soldiers came a little later to the city of Bethlehem, Jesus was not there. He was safe in Egypt, where Herod could not reach Him.

And there, until it was safe for Him to return to His own country, the little new-born King lived and grew strong and kind and loving. No-one knew He was a king. His father was a carpenter, and His friends were the boys of the villages around.

But His mother knew. Often she remembered the tale of the shepherds who had seen the angels in the sky, and she remembered too the three wise

men who had come to kneel before her baby. She
still had the wonderful presents they had given to
her for Him. He would one day be the greatest
King in the world.

But it was not by power or riches or might that the baby in the stable grew to be the greatest man the world has ever seen. It was by something greater than all these—by LOVE alone.

That is the story of the first Christmas, which we remember to this day, and which we keep with joy and delight.

·THE·END·